# Reflections

**Other Cathy® Books from Andrews and McMeel**

$14 in the bank and a $200 face in my purse
My granddaughter has fleas!!
Why do the right words always come out of the wrong mouth?
A hand to hold, an opinion to reject
Thin thighs in thirty years
Wake me up when I'm a size 5
Men should come with instruction booklets
A mouthful of breath mints and no one to kiss
Another Saturday night of wild and reckless abandon

# FIFTEENTH ANNIVERSARY

# Reflections

A *Cathy* Collection by Cathy Guisewite

**Andrews and McMeel**
A Universal Press Syndicate Company
**Kansas City**

ISBN: 0-8362-1877-9
Library of Congress Catalog Card Number: 91-73170

# Contents

# Introduction

/quit taking art class when I was seven years old because I was planning a career as a cowboy and felt it would be a waste of time to learn how to draw.

This complete lack of a grasp on reality is at least part of what's made the Cathy comic strip possible . . . an ability to march through life without a hint of what anything means at the time, matched only by an ability to torture myself about it years after it happened.

Months after a relationship is over, I can still convince myself the whole thing would have gone differently if only I'd worn a cuter pair of shoes. Weeks after a dinner party, I'm still plotting ways to eat an extra dessert without anyone noticing. Fifteen years after starting the comic strip, I'm still wishing I hadn't named the main character "Cathy."

Too embarrassing. Way too embarrassing. Especially when you consider that my first drawings were only done as part of a way to keep my feelings totally private.

My mother had always taught me to write about things instead of talking to anyone. If you're angry, she'd say, don't scream at the person. Write about it. If you're hurt or jealous, don't go gossiping to girlfriends. Write about it. If you're lonely or sad or depressed, write about it.

Over the years, this did nothing for my relationships with human beings, but I did develop a real closeness with paper. So, in 1976, when I was feeling the full confusion of having a brilliant career in advertising and a miserable love life, it was only natural for me to write about it. Anxious to let Mom know I was coping with life without speaking to anyone, I sent some illustrated versions of my anxieties home with letters. Try to imagine my horror when—after a lifetime of teaching me to keep my feelings private—she insisted my drawings were the makings of a comic strip for millions of people to enjoy.

In their earliest form, the main characters looked like this:

## CATHY

Oh Honey, Honey, Honey! I knew you'd call back! I knew you didn't mean what you said!! I KNEW it! OH, HONEY! HONEY!!!

RING RING RING

## MOM

My! You ate the entire banana-nut cake!!! You certainly must have been hungry, dear.

## ANDREA  ## IRVING

Look— you won't go to bars...
you won't go to parties...
and you won't go on a
blind date. How do you
ever expect to meet
the man of your dreams?!!

But how am I going to get
to know you if you won't
sleep with me?

Except for basic things, like trying to connect the heads to the bodies, I've never consciously changed the way the characters looked, but have always just drawn them the only way I could.

Similarly, I never set out to make the strip a voice for anything in particular, but have always just written about the things that were either happening to me or the people around me, which kind of naturally evolved into what I call the four basic guilt groups: food, love, mother, and career.

If it's strange to read the early strips now and remember how radical the concept of "women's liberation" seemed in 1976, it's just as strange to think of life before digital time, salad bars, and ATM machines. And, of course, equally strange to realize, fifteen years have passed and many of us are still having the exact same conversations with our mothers, our consciences, and the mirror in the bathing suit department.

Looking back gives us perspective on all the little, icky, scary, confusing, frustrating, and triumphant moments we've been through all alone. It gives us reassurance that, in a way, we've all been through them together. And, as we hurl into the '90s, it gives us confidence to know we have what it takes to survive whatever's coming up: hope in our hearts, and a carton of fudge ripple in the freezer.

*Cathy Guisewite*

# *Trends*

*A*re we who we are because of the stuff around us, or is the stuff around us because of who we are? If the stuff is around us because of who we are, how did we all get there at the same time? Who started it? Why do we need it? What would we have been if we hadn't had it? Why does what seemed so bizarre then seem so normal now? And what happened to my brain along the way that makes it impossible for me to sit in a chair and write this sentence if I'm not wearing running shoes?

## *1976* MILITANT LYRICS

"Our song" becomes something we sing with a girlfriend after a women's meeting.

## *1977* DIGITAL WATCHES

Precursor to the VCR revolution. People get programmed to expect that our machines will do everything except what we need them to do.

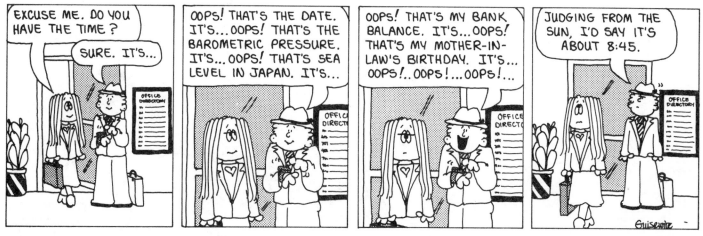

## *1978* SALAD BARS

The "Me Decade" leaves us ready to embrace the idea that we should fix our own meals at the restaurant.

## *1979* ETHNIC RESTAURANTS

Men who grew up expecting well-done roast beef cooked by a cheerful woman in an apron are now sitting on the floor eating raw fish.

## 1980 RATINGS

Men and women find a time-saving way to offend each other.

## 1981 CONVENIENCE STORES

Formerly one-per-town. Now one-per-block. Makes it infinitely more convenient to part with money, either by overspending or by being mugged.

## 1981 SURROGATES

The Vietnam War safely behind us, we begin battling it out with our desk calendars.

## *1982* RETIREMENT ACCOUNTS

Precursor to the "Publisher's Clearinghouse Sweepstakes."

## *1982* VIDEO ARCADES

What is left of our brains from 30 years of watching television is now cheerfully handed over for 25 cents a game.

## *1982* VELCRO

Introduced precisely when life-as-we-knew-it has come completely apart for many people; offers hope that things can be stuck back together, albeit temporarily.

# 1982 OPTIONS

The sexual revolution has taken middle America by storm. People go to a party looking for someone nice and leave with a group of partner-swappers wearing zodiac pendants. This phenomenon is roughly paralleled in our shopping experiences.

# 1982 VCRs

An entire country begins to grapple with the concept that we might have control over our own lives.

# 1982 MUGS

Turning point in human evolution. Having been "awakened" in so many areas, all people born after 1950 now require three times more coffee per serving to maintain our alert state than all previous civilizations have needed.

## *1982* ANSWERING MACHINES

Crime rates go up.

Panel 1: HI THERE, SWEETIE. IT'S ME. I WAS JUST THINKING ABOUT YOU AND, UH, I THOUGHT I'D SAY HELLO.

Panel 2: SO, UM...HA,HA... **HELLO!** OH, HEE, HEE, HEE... AHEM.. THIS IS STUPID.

Panel 3: NO, REALLY, I WAS JUST SITTING HERE AND HEE HEE HA, HA! **HOO HA!** WAIT... I'M.. AHEM.. **HOO HA HA HA!!**

Panel 4: EXCUSE ME, MOM. I HAVE TO GO BREAK INTO IRVING'S APARTMENT AND RIP THE TAPE OUT OF HIS PHONE ANSWERING MACHINE.

## *1982* CALCULATORS

It turns out that all that time we spent memorizing the multiplication tables in the third grade was a complete waste.

Panel 1: WE HAVE CALCULATOR CHECK-BOOKS, CALCULATOR WATCHES, CALCULATOR CREDIT CARD CASES, CALCULATOR LAMPS...

Panel 2: CALCULATOR PICTURE FRAMES, CALCULATOR PENS, CALCULATOR ATTACHÉ CASES, CALCULATOR LIGHTERS, CALCULATOR RINGS, CALCULATOR PHONES...

Panel 3: THIS YEAR WHY NOT GIVE THE GIFT OF A CALCULATOR TO EVERYONE ON YOUR LIST?

Panel 4: NOBODY I KNOW HAS ANYTHING TO ADD UP.

## *1983* MULTI-FUNCTION PHONES

Continues the training begun by digital watches; prepares us to own computers that we will use as paperweights.

Panel 1: WE HAVE THE AUTO-REDIAL TELEPHONE WITH 9, 15, OR 32-NUMBER MEMORY... THE ALL-ELECTRONIC MINI-PHONE... CORDLESS, COLLAPSIBLE OR CALCULATOR PHONES...

Panel 2: PHONES WITH A MUTE SWITCH, RINGER ON/OFF SWITCH, AND/OR AMPLIFIER SWITCH. PHONES THAT WILL ANSWER, RECORD, TIME CALLS OR TURN ELECTRICAL APPLIANCES ON OR OFF FROM ANYWHERE IN THE WORLD!

Panel 3: DO YOU HAVE ANY PHONES THAT WILL NOT RING SO MUCH AT THE OFFICE, BUT WILL RING MORE AT HOME? — NO.

Panel 4: ONCE AGAIN, MODERN TECHNOLOGY ZOOMS PAST THE OBVIOUS. PHONE CENTER

## *1983* HOME COOKING

Freshly liberated from her kitchen, modern woman discovers the satisfaction of making everything from scratch.

## *1983* HEALTH FOOD

What we start to eat when other people are watching.

## *1983* CABLE

Men sign up for it to get dates. Women sign up for it so we can watch old movies about how romantic it was before there was television.

## *1983* TRASHY LINGERIE

Mothers secretly wish we'd go back to the burning-the-bra phase.

## *1983* PASTA

The news that pasta (a forbidden food in all pre-1983 diets) might be a source of fiber, which might actually be good for us, is greeted with such jubilation that we enshrine it on our countertops.

## *1983* GOURMET FATTENING FOOD

Strategically introduced just before the workout revolution, in a cunning, yet successful attempt to make sure no new members will ever achieve their "desired weight loss."

## 1983 BEEFCAKE

Our mothers get their first good look at a man who isn't our father.

## 1984 BOIL-IN-BAG MEALS

Women discover a driving competitive spirit, even though we didn't play team sports as children.

## 1984 THEME CHECKS

Another "Me Decade" holdover. Just in case someone didn't read our mugs, T-shirts, or bumper stickers, we find it necessary to make identity statements while paying bills.

## *1984* **MICROWAVES**

Woman further frees herself from a kitchen she never goes into.

## *1984* **MONOGAMY**

Except for the pasta-as-diet-food concept, the first good news our mothers have had in several years.

## *1984* **PRE-NUPTIALS**

Women who have started earning their own money are no longer as comfortable with the concept of sharing everything.

## 1985 SINGLE-SERVING ENTRÉES

In the wake of the sexual revolution, many of us find we are now making the exact same kinds of decisions about our food as we are about our love lives.

## 1985 DESIGNER LABELS

The people who label us "yuppies" are just jealous because we have cover stories in *Newsweek* and *Time*.

# *1985* DESIGNER FOOD

(*see*: DESIGNER LABELS)

# *1985* DESIGNER COFFEE

(*see*: DESIGNER FOOD)

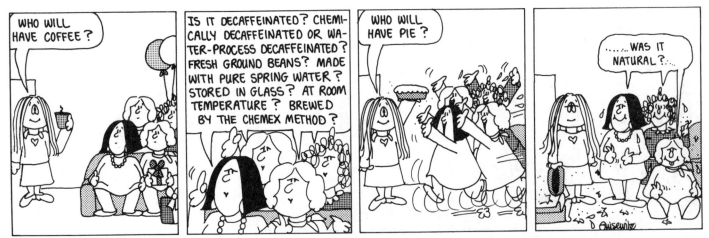

# *1985* DESIGNER KITCHENS

(*see*: DESIGNER COFFEE)

# *1985* DESIGNER WATER

(*see*: DESIGNER KITCHENS)

## *1985* DESIGNER CARRY-OUT

(*see*: DESIGNER WATER)

## *1985* MAGAZINE SWEEPSTAKES

Coincidentally enough, it becomes normal to find a chance to win $1,000,000 in the same mailbox as a $1000 VISA bill.

# *1985* CALL WAITING

For those of us who have not alienated all our friends and relatives with our answering machines, a chance to alienate them in person.

# *1985* MERCHANDISING

The very people who are "sick of all the Star Wars stuff" will have a stuffed Garfield suction-cupped to their car window within 18 months.

# *1985* PERSONAL COMPUTERS

We don't know why, but we want one.

## *1985* PERSONAL ORGANIZATION SYSTEMS

Cashing in on the human spirit, people create entire stores full of color-coordinated ways to organize our lives that don't involve the personal computers we just bought.

## *1985* BOARD GAMES

Beginning of the "cocooning trend": bored with going out and boasting about what we own, couples discover the fun of staying inside and boasting about what we know.

24

## 1986 HEALTH CLUBS

Singles' bar of the '80s.

## 1986 TANNING BOOTHS

The *pièce de résistance* of the Hedonism Decade. Notable not only because we're now paying for something every human on earth had previously gotten for free . . . but because by the time the last historical site has been bulldozed to make room for the last mini-mall containing the last tanning booth, tanning of any kind will be declared unsafe, unhealthy, and totally uncool.

## *1986* TRANSFORMERS

Adults who are trying to be five things at once begin buying toys for their children that will encourage them to think this is normal.

## *1986* CLOSETS

We begin to lust after the one and only thing we haven't been able to buy.

# 1986 PORTABLE DESK ACCESSORIES

Liberated from our desks by time-saving devices, we now carry the rest of our office with us wherever we go.

# 1986 HOME ENTERTAINMENT CENTERS

We begin to measure how solid someone's relationship is by how much stuff is plugged in in the den.

## 1986 SOUND

The generation that introduced ear-shattering music to the world somehow becomes the expert on the subtle nuances of sound.

## 1986 HARDWARE STORES

The personal computer industry continues to miss the point.

# *1986* OVERNIGHT DELIVERY

Mail carriers now work full-time delivering contest entries, advertisements, and mail-order catalogs. Any really important "mail" goes by an overnight service.

# *1986* RELATIONSHIP BOOKS

Where all women's money went before there was a Victoria's Secret in every mall.

# 1986 IN-STORE SECURITY

Just in case it wasn't hideous enough to try on bathing suits and lingerie, women now get an audience.

# 1987 OVERBOOKING

Knowing how blasé people have become about the adventure of travel, airlines try making the experience more interesting by selling twice as many tickets as they have seats on the plane.

# 1987 POWER LUNCH

"Lunch" becomes something you stuff in your mouth on the way to something else.

## 1987 CAMCORDERS

A whole new way to look at our parents.

## 1987 PROMISCUOUS COLOGNE

Our cologne starts having more fun than we are.

## 1987 CHARGE CARDS

Coincidentally enough, just as people start paying for everything with someone else's money, we start buying things for someone else's life.

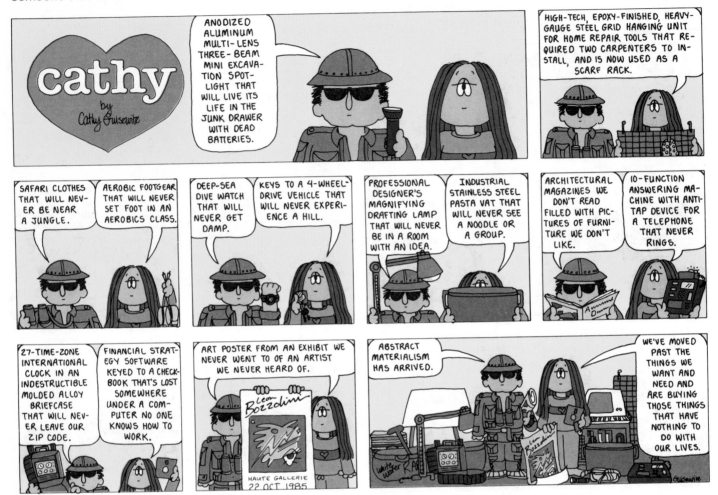

## 1987 SELF-RIGHTEOUSNESS

Running out of things to buy, the baby boom generation puts a down payment on the high moral ground.

## *1988* WRINKLE CURES

The young people find another way to aggravate our mothers by "reinventing" wrinkles and wrinkle cures.

## *1987* UNISEX

"Boys will be boys" and "Girls will be girls" are passé expressions. People, however, will still be people.

# *1988* BONUS POINTS

The one and only reason any of us will still agree to go on business trips.

# *1988* NEW AGE

Committed to coolness, the baby boomers find a way to describe what's happening to us besides "turning into grandma."

# 1988 SPF'S

All the money we spent on aerosol hairspray in 1960 is now spent protecting ourselves from the hole we squirted in the ozone.

# 1988 INTELLIGENT TOYS

Babies prove they're still smarter than any of us.

# 1988 HAIR CARE SYSTEMS

What we buy to make sure we still don't have any free time.

# 1988 CATALOGS

Just in case we can't get to the mall, we find a way to go broke from our kitchens and desks.

# 1988 BAILOUTS

Workaholics start coming to their senses and becoming relaxaholics.

## 1989 FIBER

Now deeply reinvested in monogamy, we find other ways to add total confusion to our lives.

## 1989 FAUX

By using the French spelling of "phony," taste-setters of the world convince those of us who haven't gone bankrupt yet that it is *très chic* to spend a fortune on copies.

## *1989* UNCONSTRUCTED FURNITURE

The "instant gratification" generation spends millions on furniture we can *take home immediately*, even though it means we have to build it ourselves.

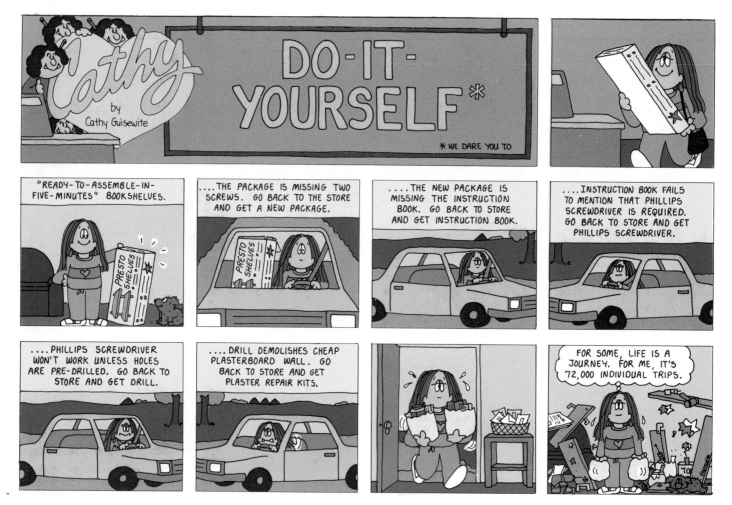

## *1989* PULL-OUT RADIOS

Sick of being made fools of by burglars, we indignantly begin marching into restaurants, offices, and parties carrying parts of our cars.

## *1989* X-RATED ADVERTISING

"Wholesome family values" are back. We rejoice that there's still a way to horrify our mothers.

## *1989* PAPER BAGS

The ordering-in food business booms as going to the grocery store becomes one moral dilemma after another.

## *1990* MOTIVATIONAL TAPES

In case we didn't have enough to be annoyed about in rush-hour traffic, someone suggests we use the time to study French, hone our business skills, and do isometric butt exercises.

# *1990* FUND-RAISERS

Singles' bar of the '90s. Approximately $150-more-of-a-bummer per evening if you leave without meeting anyone.

# *1990* HIGH-TECH MEDICAL EQUIPMENT

Under the guise of "caring for the temple which is his body," the aging baby boomer finds a way to make it hip to carry a heart-rate monitor when he goes for a walk.

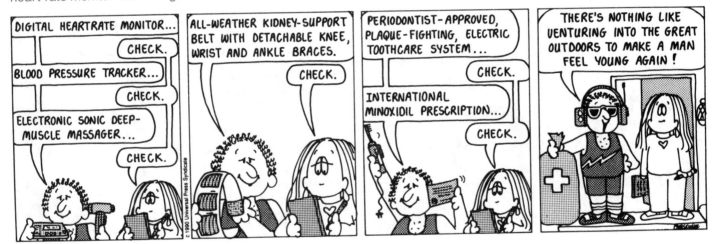

# *1990* IN-STORE BOUTIQUES

Having spent the last twenty years tearing down all the cute little specialty shops to make way for giant department store malls, the giant department stores start building cute little specialty shops.

## *1990* ENVIRONMENTAL AWARENESS

For some, a movement. For some, a new sport.

## *1990* BANKRUPTCY

Those of us who spent 1989 ridiculing Donald Trump begin identifying with him.

## *1990* POWER SALADS

No longer something that just "comes with dinner," salads now take up half the menu and cost as much as a steak.

# 1990 ATM MACHINES

Metaphor for the '90s relationship. Just when we're ready to completely trust one, we can't find one that works.

# 1991 LUGGAGE

Formerly something we packed when leaving town; now required for daily life.

42

## *1990* GROUP ANONYMITY

One of a person's main forms of identity becomes which "anonymous" support groups he or she belongs to.

## *1991* INSTANTANEOUS COMMUNICATION

With every new technological breakthrough, it takes longer to reach a human being.

# *1991* LINES

Where all the time we're saving gets spent.

# *1991* ECO-GUILT

Over-commercialized and over-computerized, the nation rediscovers the simple, honest pleasure of blaming someone else.

# Women

*B*y 1976, the first sex discrimination case had been filed,
the first nationwide Women's Strike for Equality had happened,
the first all-woman's pro tennis tour had taken place,
the first women generals had been commissioned,
the first girls had been appointed as senate pages,
the first woman had been ordained a rabbi,
the first women's studies courses were being offered,
the first affirmative action hiring plans were in place,
the first girls had gotten to play in Little League,
the first female president of a major university had been named,
the first woman had climbed Mount Everest,
the first commercials had been pulled off the air because of "sexism,"
the first women had been named *Time* magazine's Man of the Year,
"Ms." had a place in the dictionary,
and Billie Jean King had beaten Bobby Riggs at tennis.

A lot had already happened.

A lot of us found ourselves floundering between two ideals—the "liberated woman" and the "traditional woman"—with absolutely no idea how to integrate the two.

These were exhilarating, but trying, times for middle America. So much of what is taken for granted today was brand new to many of us then, and the role models were all such extremes. You could either be a "women's libber" or be "just like your mother." There was a support group for everything but the middle ground; those lost souls who, like me, were in complete agreement with both sides of the argument at once.

I coped with the contradictions I was feeling by creating two characters . . . Andrea, who was always the champion of the new way, and Cathy, who—except when she was talking to her mother—rooted for the old.

At the time, no one was talking about "having it all." To many people, being pro-women implied you were anti-men, especially since the qualities required to revolutionize the attitudes of a whole nation weren't exactly the dainty flirtatious ones.

In the first year of the strip, Andrea led Cathy through Transcendental Meditation, a Women-of-Today Club, and an Assertiveness Training Workshop, all with pretty much the same results.

The women's movement was part of what came to be called the "Me Decade" . . . a time when, in our own way, we each embarked on a rich, personal journey to question what we'd been and find out who we were.

We searched for our voices . . .

We searched for new identities . . .

We searched for answers . . .

We reveled in our independence . . .

We rejected our independence . . .

48

We fell in love with the future . . .

We mourned the past . . .

We discovered having it all . . .

We discovered having nothing . . .

We lashed out at life . . .

Life lashed back . . .

We got in touch with our feelings . . .

We got in touch with our bodies . . .

We got in touch with our potential . . .

We earned the respect of our peers . . .

We earned the respect of ourselves . . .

Until finally, having embraced the concept that everything was within our grasp, having tasted success in all areas of life, we began to notice that no matter how much we were doing, someone else was doing more, and doing it better.

It isn't that the new role models haven't been inspiring. When I hear about a woman who has it totally together careerwise, I'm inspired, I'm proud, and I go home and eat a carton of Cool Whip. When I hear about a woman who has a perfect career and a perfect relationship with an intelligent, sensitive man, I go home, eat the Cool Whip, and scream at my date. When I hear about a woman who has a perfect career, a perfect relationship, two adorable bilingual children, and has regular open, loving chats with her mother about their sex lives, I write out my frustrations in M&M's and eat them, one paragraph at a time.

In theory, we all say we've rejected the notion of being Superwoman. In practice, I don't know anyone who isn't still trying. On the following pages are samples of what at least some of us have gone through in our attempt to do it all . . .

55

58

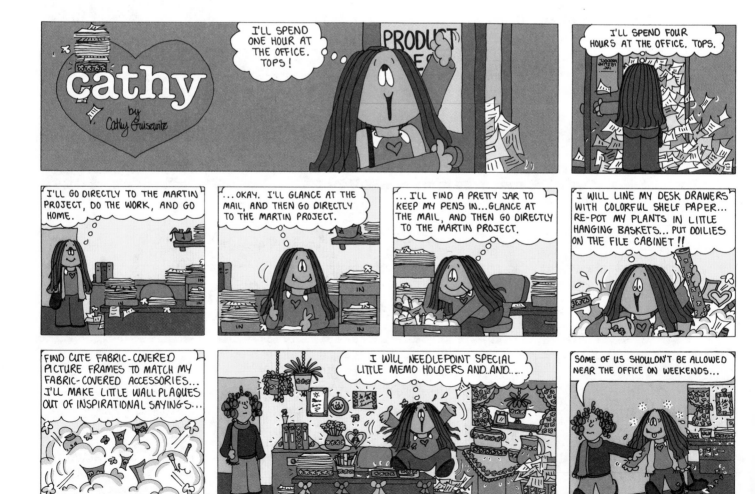

# Men

*M*arried people ask me why Cathy's still with Irving. Single people who are in wonderful relationships ask me why Cathy's still with Irving. Single people who saw someone cute in the grocery store last night, and are already scheming to buy all future groceries at 8:45 on Tuesday evenings just in case he's there again, ask why Cathy's still with Irving.

I'm told that after a woman has a baby her body releases a hormone that makes her forget what giving birth was really like, which, in turn, makes it possible for there to be another generation of children. I'm convinced that a similar hormone is released the second someone thinks she's in, or on the brink of, a good relationship. I call this the hope hormone. It remains in the body the entire time you're with someone, convincing you that if things don't work out, there will always be someone else . . . making some people even eager to experience all the someone elses that are out there . . . In any case, also acting to ensure there will be another generation by making people want to at least try having a relationship with someone in this one.

The hope hormone usually disappears entirely within the first fifteen seconds of a blind date.

Thus, people who are really single—single as in no steady dates, no potential steady dates, no meaningful eye contact for at least six months, people who are not single by choice but who are single because EACH AND EVERY PERSON THEY FIND ATTRACTIVE IS ALREADY MARRIED, ENGAGED, LIVING WITH SOMEONE, OR ATTRACTED TO THE SAME MEN SHE IS—these people don't ask why Cathy's still with Irving.

The experience of trying to meet someone else is way too fresh in their memories.

For people who have forgotten what dating was like then, or any time since, I offer a sampling of Cathy's first—and often last—encounters with men who weren't Irving.

## *1976* JOHN

## *1977* EMERSON

## *1978* ERNIE

## 1979 PHILLIP

## 1979 WALTER

67

## 1979 CHARLES

## 1980 RON

## 1981 HOWARD

## 1981 TED

## 1981 DONALD

## 1981 RICHARD, PHILLIP, TOM, STEVE, GREG, HENRY, BILL, MARK, BRIAN, TIM, JOHN, BOB, FRED, RON, AND JOEY

## 1981 TOM

## 1982 DANIEL

Panel 1: IF I KISS THIS MAN GOODNIGHT, I WILL ENCOURAGE HIM AND I'M NOT SURE I WANT TO DO THAT.

Panel 2: THEN AGAIN, IF I DON'T KISS HIM, IT WILL BE DEVASTATING TO HIS EGO AND WILL PROBABLY RUIN HIS WHOLE WEEK.

Panel 3: I'D BETTER KISS HIM. JUST ONE, LITTLE, TEENSY KISS...

OKAY WITH YOU IF I JUST SPEND THE NIGHT?

Panel 4: WHY AM I ALWAYS HAVING THE WRONG CONVERSATION?

## 1982 FRANK

cathy
by Cathy Guisewite

Panel: COME HERE OFTEN?

Panel: NOT OFTEN ENOUGH.

Panel: TELL ME ABOUT YOURSELF, CATHY. — WELL, LET'S SEE...

Panel: I'M THE PRODUCT OF TWO GENERATIONS, FRANK. I HAVE ALL THE ANXIETIES OF MY MOTHER'S GENERATION, PLUS ALL THE ANXIETIES OF MY GENERATION.

Panel: I'M JUGGLING TWO GENERATIONS OF VALUES, TWO GENERATIONS OF DREAMS, AND TWO GENERATIONS OF GUILT.

Panel: HA, HA! I WILL **AMAZE** YOU, FRANK! I WILL **INSPIRE** YOU! I WILL AWE YOU WITH MY DETERMINATION AND DRIVE BUT **HA, HA** OH YES, FRANK, I **WILL** CONFUSE YOU!!

Panel: TELL ME ABOUT YOURSELF, CATHY. — I LOVE SPORTS.

## 1982 GREG

## 1982 GRANT

## 1982 GRANT

## 1982 RON

## 1983 PETER

74

## 1983 HAROLD

## 1983 ERNEST

## *1984* JEFF

## *1984* ERNEST

## *1984* MITCHELL

## 1985 MAX

**Panel 1:** WELL, HERE'S MY LIVING SPACE, CATHY... CONDO, SWEET CONDO!

**Panel 2:** HERE'S MY PC, MY VCR, MY WORKOUT EQUIPMENT, MY RELAXATION TANK, MY AUDIO SYSTEM, MY COMMUNICATION CENTER, MY WORK STATION....

**Panel 3:** I DON'T KNOW WHAT TO SAY, MAX. / DON'T SAY ANYTHING. I KNOW JUST WHAT YOU'RE THINKING.

**Panel 4:** THERE'S NO ROOM FOR ANY OF MY STUFF IN HERE.

## 1985 JAKE

**Panel 1:** cathy by Cathy Guisewite — CLICK! WHIRR.... — BEEP! BZZZZ...

**Panel 2:** BEEP! BZZZ... CLICK! ZOOP! WHIRR... CLICK! WHIRR... ZOOP!

**Panel 3:** AS SOON AS OUR EYES MET I KNEW YOU WERE SOMEONE I'D LIKE TO EXCHANGE TAPES WITH, CATHY. YOU ARE ON VHS, AREN'T YOU? / NO. BETA.

**Panel 4:** YOU'RE BETA?? / YOU'RE VHS??

**Panel 5:** IT DOESN'T MATTER. ALL THAT COUNTS IS THAT YOUR SOFTWARE IS WRITTEN TO CPM/86. / NO... NO... ...MINE'S MS/DOS.

**Panel 6:** WE CAN OVERCOME ANYTHING...JUST PLEASE SAY YOUR AUDIO SYSTEM IS COMPACT LASER DISC. / HIGH BIAS CASSETTES.

**Panel 7:** IT'S OKAY...WE'LL LEAVE HERE! WE'LL TRAVEL TOGETHER!! / YES! WE CAN TRAVEL!

**Panel 8:** WE'LL GATHER BONUS POINTS TOGETHER ON AMERICAN AIRLINES! / NO!...DARLING! MY POINTS ARE ON UNITED!!

**Panel 9:** WAAAH! IF ONLY WE'D MET IN ANOTHER TIME!!

**Panel 10:** INCOMPATIBLE OPERATING SYSTEMS HAVE TAKEN OVER WHERE RELIGIOUS DIFFERENCES LEFT OFF.

## 1985 SANDY

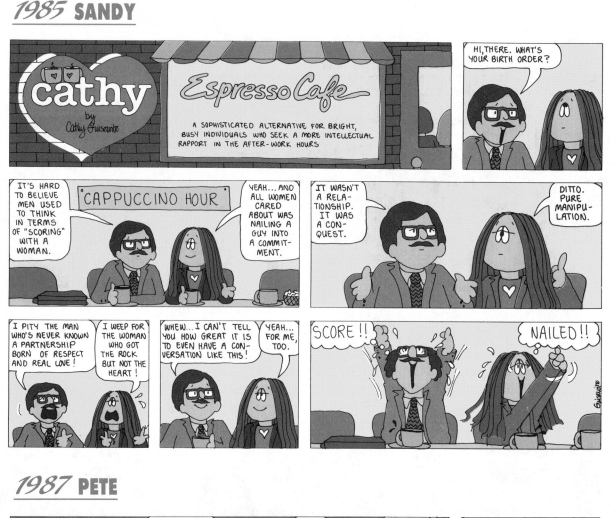

## 1987 PETE

## 1988 VAN

## 1988 MITCH

## 1988 LEONARD

## 1988 GENE

## 1989 BRADLEY

## 1989 KEVIN

## 1989 GERALD

## *1990* SIMON

## *1990* MARK

# Meeting Men

*A* t last count, there were 25,893,342 bright, beautiful, vibrant, charming, accomplished eligible single women for every vaguely acceptable eligible single man. The fact that this statistic came from the lips of a weary—"BUT NOT DESPERATE!"—forty-year-old single girlfriend says a lot about what the single experience continues to be for women.

Way too much of it is spent with other women. Way too much of it is spent with other women in women's stores. Way, way too much of it is spent with other women reading women's magazines before going into women's stores.

One teensy portion of it gets spent actually attempting to meet a man.

A few brave souls, like Cathy, have actually tried some of the things everyone talks about and, if nothing else, have provided a role model for the rest of us of things to not do ourselves.

## *1976* VIDEO DATING

## *1977* BARS

## *1978* TAKING THE INITIATIVE

## 1979 LYING

## 1980 GROCERY SHOPPING

## *1981* COMMISERATING WITH GIRLFRIENDS

## *1982* TAKING THE INITIATIVE

## *1983* QUESTIONING THE UNIVERSE

## *1983* TAKING THE INITIATIVE

## *1984* PERSONAL ADS

## 1984 PERSONAL ADS

## 1984 PERSONAL ADS

## 1984 PERSONAL ADS

## *1984* **PERSONAL ADS**

## *1984* **COMMISERATING WITH GIRLFRIENDS**

## *1984* **SELF-IMPROVEMENT CLASSES**

## 1985 HEALTH CLUBS

## 1985 BARS

## 1985 COMMISERATING WITH GIRLFRIENDS

## *1985* COMPUTER INTERFACING

## *1986* COMMISERATING WITH GIRLFRIENDS

## *1986* COMMISERATING WITH GIRLFRIENDS

## 1986 AVOIDANCE

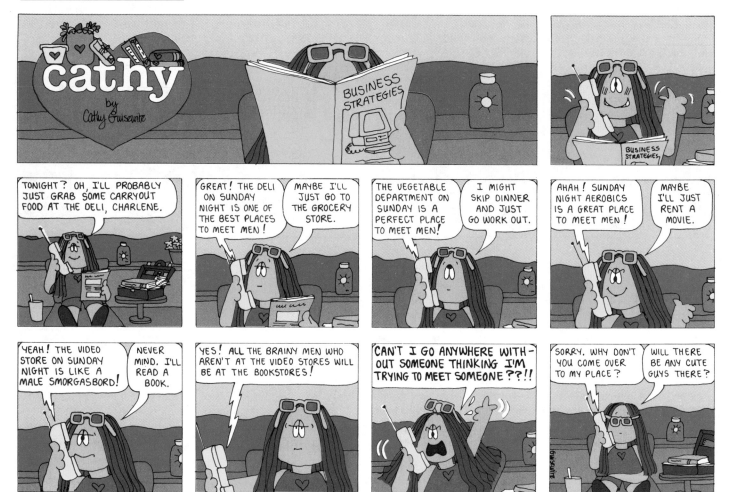

## 1987 WATCHING TV

## *1987* DENIAL

## *1987* HEALTH CLUBS

## *1987* GROCERY SHOPPING

## *1987* PARTIES

## *1987* COMMISERATING WITH GIRLFRIENDS

## *1987* REJECTION

## *1987* COMMISERATING WITH GIRLFRIENDS

## *1988* GROCERY SHOPPING

## 1988 LIST-MAKING

## 1988 BLIND DATES

## 1988 OFFICE ENCOUNTERS

## *1989* STUDYING TALK SHOW GUESTS

## *1989* STUDYING BOOKS

## *1989* PARTIES

## *1989* BLIND DATES

## *1989* MINGLING

101

## *1989* COMMISERATING WITH GIRLFRIENDS

## *1989* FAX MACHINES

## *1989* BACHELOR AUCTIONS

## *1989* COMMISERATING WITH GIRLFRIENDS

## *1989* COMMISERATING WITH GIRLFRIENDS

## *1989* SLEEPING

HI THERE!

GET REAL.

IT ALWAYS GOES BACK TO THE SAME OLD THING, CHARLENE...

A WOMAN CAN'T ATTRACT REAL LOVE UNLESS SHE LOVES HERSELF FIRST.

WE LOVE OURSELVES, CATHY.

WE LOVE OURSELVES ENOUGH TO REJECT A GEEK, BUT NOT ENOUGH TO SUSTAIN SOMETHING WITH SOMEONE GREAT.

AS SOON AS WE'RE WITH SOMEONE GREAT, WE START TO WAVER ON HOW MUCH WE LOVE OURSELVES.

WE WAVER ON WHETHER OR NOT WE'RE REALLY WORTHY... AND GET SO INSECURE, PARANOID AND WEIRD THAT WE TRASH ANY HOPE OF MAKING THE RELATIONSHIP WORK!

WE HAVE THE COMMITMENT PROBLEM, CHARLENE! MEN ARE NOT TO BLAME! WE WOMEN HAVE A COMMITMENT PROBLEM WITH OURSELVES!

I HATE MYSELF FOR THINKING UP THAT ONE.

EVERY HOUR I SPEND WITH YOU IS ANOTHER $200 I'LL HAVE TO SPEND ON MY THERAPIST.

I THOUGHT YOU SAID SIMON WAS PERFECT.

ON DATE NO. 1, I THOUGHT HE WAS PERFECT, CHARLENE.

ON DATE NO. 2, I THOUGHT HE WAS PERFECT.

ON DATE NO. 3, I NOTICED THAT HE'S AN ARROGANT, EGOTISTICAL WHINER, WITH AN ANNOYING SENSE OF HUMOR, BORING STORIES, OBSESSIVE DINING HABITS...THAT HIS HEAD SMELLS LIKE STYLING GEL, AND HE WEARS HIS SOCKS INSIDE OUT!

I CAN'T BELIEVE THIS, CATHY.

I KNOW. IF I'M EVER GOING TO GET MARRIED, IT'S GOING TO HAVE TO BE ON THE SECOND DATE.

## *1990* STEALING GIRLFRIENDS' REJECTS

## *1990* COMMISERATING WITH GIRLFRIENDS

### 1991 VIDEO DATING

### 1991 VIDEO DATING

### 1991 BEGGING FOR MORE TIME

# *Irving*

If I've been able to write effectively about relationships, it's because I've never had a clue what was going on in any of my own, and was more than happy to pass this trait on to Cathy. Cathy's boyfriend, Irving, has been a perfect counterpoint for her in this way, because he's never had a clue what was going on either.

Because I've never wanted Irving to represent anyone in particular, I've always tried to make the strips with Irving be much more about Cathy's reaction to him than about Irving himself. Not to mention the fact that I could never presume to guess what was really going on inside the male brain.

How is it that men can be so confusing, while we women always say exactly what's on our minds?

How is it that men can be so frustrating, while we women are so reasonable?

**107**

How is it that men can be so elusive, while women are so clear about our needs?

How is it that men are still so totally impossible to figure out?

What we do know about Irving is that he grew up in a time when his entire conditioning had prepared him to be with the type of woman who had pretty much ceased to exist the second he was old enough to meet her. He's gone through a lot of transitions since then, some more voluntarily than others.

## *1976* THE GETTING-TO-KNOW-YOU PHASE

## *1977* THE ENLIGHTENMENT PHASE

## *1978* THE SEXUAL LIBERATION PHASE

## *1979* THE RESENTMENT PHASE

## *1980* THE TOGETHERNESS PHASE

## *1981* THE SENSITIVITY PHASE

## *1982* THE RETURN-TO-ROMANCE PHASE

## *1983* THE MONOGAMY PHASE

## *1984* THE OVERACHIEVER PHASE

## 1985 THE INNOCENCE PHASE

## 1986 THE LOSS-OF-POWER PHASE

## 1987 THE REINSTATEMENT-OF-POWER PHASE

## *1988* THE COMMUNICATION PHASE

## *1989* THE PHYSICAL FITNESS PHASE

## *1990* THE SELF-AWARENESS PHASE

The one clear beauty of being single is that you can just go home when you get sick of each other. Except for that, every couple I know—married or not—has at least a little bit of Cathy and Irving's relationship in their own. A delicate balance of total devotion and complete disgust . . . a spirit of loving unity mixed with an utter incomprehension of how the other one thinks . . . a passion that will last a lifetime combined with that nagging little question of whether or not they actually want to see each other again.

What follows are some of the high points, some of the low points, and many of the who-knows-what's-going-on points, of Cathy and Irving's relationship.

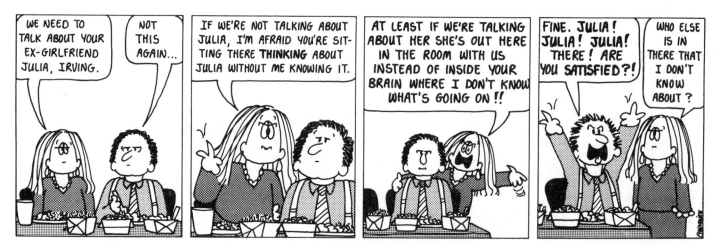

149

# Mom

*L*ike many enlightened, intelligent women of my generation, I have learned to look deep within myself and blame everything that ever happened to me on my mother.

Since the comic strip began . . . fifteen years of intense self-analysis, thousands of conversations, and millions of hours of searching introspection later, my relationship with Mom has evolved from this in the '70s . . .

. . . to this, last year . . .

**151**

While I have staunchly maintained my role as a six-year-old in our relationship, Mom has changed with the times . . . making, for instance, the transition through the sexual revolution as graciously as possible for someone who had June Cleaver as a role model.

## 1976 MOM ON "YOU KNOW WHAT"

## 1982 MOM ON "YOU KNOW WHAT"

## 1984 MOM ON "YOU KNOW WHAT"

None of the relationships in the strip are as intense, or as closely quoted from real life. I can do this partly because my mother has a wonderful sense of humor about herself, and partly because—when the sense of humor doesn't kick in—she has an amazing capacity for complete denial, allowing her to instantly blame all the "touchy" ones on Aunt Rena.

I am, of course, simultaneously thrilled and horrified to see these same qualities in myself.

If the women's movement made those of us who were twenty years old in 1970 confused, it made our mothers berserk. Not only because it challenged every single aspect of how they'd lived their lives, but because it did it at the precise moment they thought they could finally sit back, admire their life achievement—which was us—and wait for the grandchildren to start happening.

It wasn't that Mom didn't agree with the "liberated woman" concept . . . more that she had a whole life and ten thousand mother/daughter speeches invested in the other system. As a result, every single new idea both inspired and offended my mother to the exact same degree. She became a bundle of contradictions; a woman who sent me a subscription to *Ms* magazine in the same envelope as a six-part series she had clipped and laminated from *Woman's Day* on "The Perfect Bride."

It was a rich addition to the foundation of contradiction our relationship was already built on, which—even to this day—makes it possible for us to have an argument, switch sides in the middle, and continue the argument without missing a beat.

In retrospect, those of us who were in our twenties only had to shift our expectations. Our mothers had to shake up their whole lives. Lots of them got divorced, lots went back to school, lots started working. Some astounding overachievers, like my own mother, discovered a way to keep being exactly who they were while being someone entirely different.

In 1979, Cathy's mom read *The Women's Room* and formed her own consciousness-raising group.

In 1980, Mom's consciousness-raising group formed a temporary help service, which later became a dating service.

By 1988, the group had dwindled to two and evolved into a personal trainer business . . .

. . . which quickly evolved into a personal trainer/muffin business.

Cathy's relationship with Mom continues to be a rich tangle of love, anxiety, togetherness, rebellion, devotion, frustration, friendship, and hysteria. I write about Cathy's father much less than her mother, at least partly because I've always wanted to be sure I had one parent at home that I wasn't alienating on any given day. Even though Dad says less in the strip, I think it's clear that he's a very important factor in Cathy's life . . . and that he often functions in the critical role that my own father does: helping me keep my sense of humor about Mom.

If Cathy, Mom, and Dad were capable of ever getting a scrapbook together, these would be some of the highlights of the last fifteen years . . .

159

168

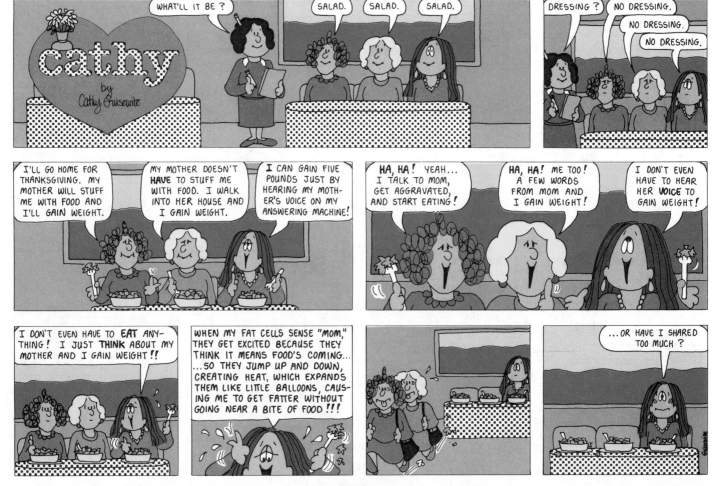

178

# Fashion

*W*ith every glorious new set of images for women has come another whole wardrobe that's required.

It used to be we needed two kinds of clothes: casual and dressy. Suddenly, we're dynamic business people, nurturing homemakers, sultry sex kittens, community leaders, romantic soul mates, athletic wonders, and global activists, all within the same week. Not only do we now need casual and dressy outfits with matching shoes for each and every image . . . but a large enough variety of sizes, so we're not caught in the awkward position of having to wear a power suit on a day when the only thing that fits is the earth-mother frock.

If this weren't distressing enough, even "casual" and "dressy" have multiplied in meaning to the point where many formerly charismatic women are choosing to simply stay at home in a bathrobe.

I'm sometimes criticized for reinforcing the superficial stereotype of woman-as-shopper by doing so many shopping strips, but my feeling is that the wardrobe situation is really a microcosm of life as a woman. . . . That, while a man can grab a pair of black socks and be done with it, almost every area of a woman's life is complicated by a wall of options not unlike the pantyhose section in the department store.

Of course, it isn't just pantyhose. Every part of our bodies has a whole set of expectations to live up to—from the color of our eyelids to the height of the heels on our shoes—and way too many options for how to do it. Even women who hate to shop have to spend a lot more time and money shopping than men do, just to look acceptable.

While I have personally used my findings to rationalize buying almost any amount of clothing, I think it's important for everyone to have some compassion about the requirements women face, to understand that much of the time it isn't self-indulgence, just part of the deal . . . and, I think, fairly symbolic of the different experience that life is for women and men.

Most of the men I know found a look they liked when they were ten years old and have pretty much worn the exact same look ever since. Most of the women I know have not. Like trying all the same diets, the looks we've been through unite us, give us a history together. A woman could walk up to a woman she'd never met on the street, say the words "body stocking," and have an instant bond with someone who—chances are—also still hasn't fully recovered from the experience, or figured out a discreet way to stuff hers into the Goodwill box.

In the last fifteen years, this is some of what we've been through:

## *1976* THE WRINKLED LOOK

## *1977* THE LAYERED LOOK

## *1978* FRENCH JEANS

## *1979* DESIGNER POLYESTER

## *1979* SLIT SKIRTS

## *1979* BUILT-IN-PANTY PANTY HOSE

## 1979 VELOUR

## 1980 THE "DRESS FOR SUCCESS" LOOK

## 1981 STRETCH JEANS

## 1982 THE PRAIRIE LOOK

## 1983 LEOTARDS

## 1984 TEXTURED PANTY HOSE

## *1985* SHOULDER PADS

## *1985* INDOOR BOOTS

## *1985* SPANDEX

## *1985* MORE LAYERS

## *1985* BODY STOCKINGS

## *1986* LINGERIE

## *1988* **CHAOS**

## *1988* **MODESTY**

## *1988* **MENSWEAR**

## *1989* CHIFFON

## *1989* THE WRAP

## *1989* LOGO CLOTHING

## *1989* VESTS

## *1990* TANK TOPS

## *1990* SHORTS SUITS

## *1990* ECOLOGICAL CORRECTNESS

## *1991* THE PATTERNED TIGHTS, OVERSIZED TOP LOOK

## *1991* UNITARDS

## *1991* THE HYPOCRITE LOOK

## *1991* MICRO-MINIS

## *1991* DRESSES

## 1991 ARTIFICIAL EVERYTHING

## 1991 RETRO-FASHION

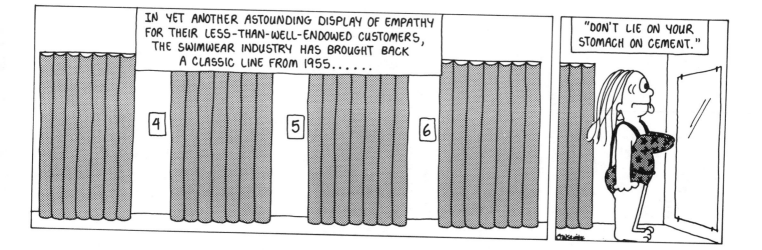

In 1976 Cathy met up with one particular salesclerk, and hasn't been able to shake her since. This same woman is not only the clerk in almost every store Cathy goes into, but the insurance agent, real estate broker, travel agent, supermarket clerk, bank teller, IRS counselor . . . basically anyone who's in a position to aggravate her.

In keeping with the meticulous planning of all the characters in the strip, she became this universal symbol for the interchangeable face of bureaucracy, because this was the only way I could draw an aggravating-looking woman.

In the '70s, when I was just finding my voice, she was always the annoying one.

By the '90s, I had found my voice, and realized I was just as annoying as she was.

In the years between, she's been involved in almost every area of Cathy's life, but never more near and dear to my own heart as when she's playing the role of the department store clerk.

211

# Diets

*W*hat can I say about Cathy's diet except that, fifteen years later, she's still on it.

What can I say about my own diet except that, having weighed fifty pounds more than I do now for way too long a time, I know the damage I'm capable of.

The very fact that I can look through fifteen years of dieting strips and remember what I was eating when I wrote almost every single one of them should give some clue as to why food has the importance in Cathy's life that it does.

The fact that the very first comic strip I ever wrote was about food is, I guess, appropriate. I was sitting in my kitchen, writing depressing things in my diary and eating everything in sight while I waited for the man of my dreams who never called to call. I only drew the picture because I was several hours into a sugar overload and had reached that giddy stage of total despair when humor and tragedy smash into each other head-on. Even though I couldn't draw, I felt compelled to elaborate on my misery by seeing the scene in picture form.

Inspired by how happy it made me to see a picture of myself at my worst, I began spending lots of evenings eating and drawing, slowly compiling a little pile of 4500-calorie "slices of life," which I started sending home with letters to my parents just to let them know I had some shred of humor intact. My mother eventually forced me to send the drawings to a comic strip syndicate, which is the only reason Cathy exists in the newspaper instead of being flung into one of the cardboard boxes of "miscellaneous treasured family mementos" in Mom's and Dad's storage room. I now realize that by making me get my work syndicated, Mom was cleverly eliminating one thing she'd have to organize when they finally get around to "tackling the room."

Since my entire art training took place at that kitchen table, the majority of my brain still believes that food is a critical part of the creative process. To this day, every time I face a blank piece of paper, it's in there chanting that I'd be able to think of a joke if I ate a doughnut. I could probably whip off a week's work if I had a bag of chocolate chip cookies in front of me . . . If I had a quart of ice cream on the desk, imagine what I could . . .

This is at least partly why Cathy has never exactly achieved total dieting success. For most of us, the struggle changes with the times, but never actually goes away. If it's possible to have "highlights" of a diet, these are some of Cathy's.

## *1977* THE DIET

## *1978* THE DIET

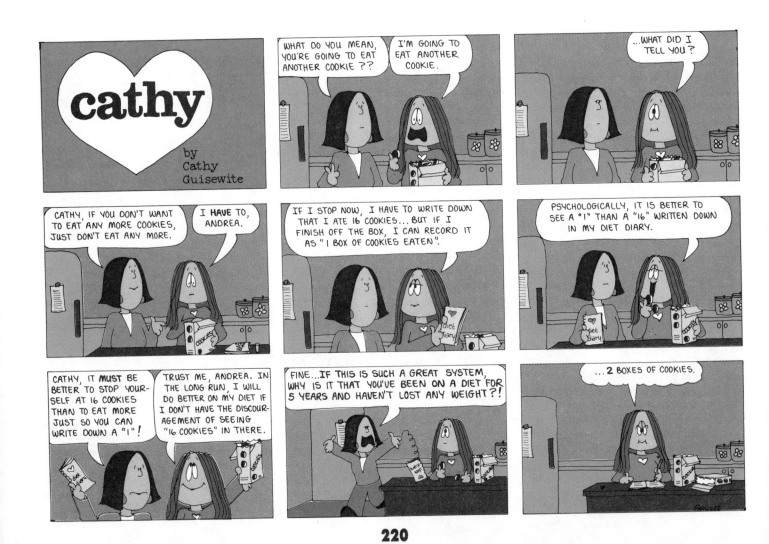

221

## 1984 THE DIET

## 1985 THE DIET

## 1986 THE DIET

233

237

241

## *1990* THE DIET

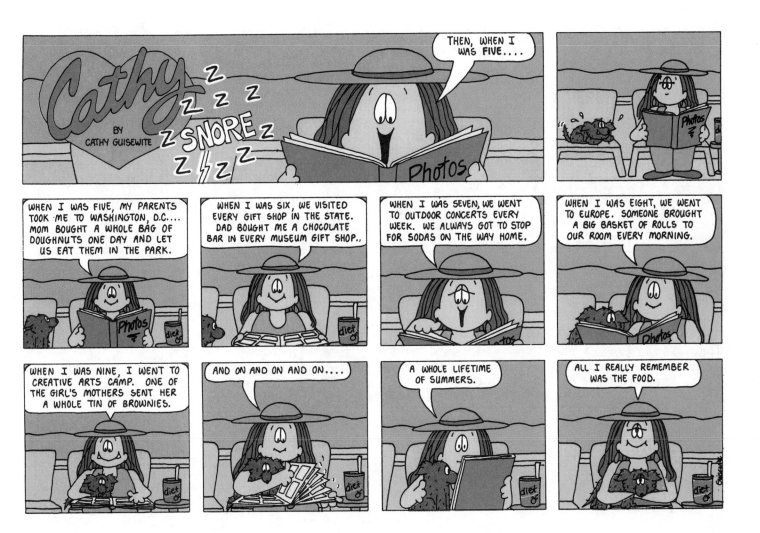

## 1991 THE DIET

# *Motherhood*

*S*ometime around 1983, many dynamic, driven, successful, trail-blazing, career Wonder Women looked up from our desks long enough to notice that something else had been going on while we were at the office every weekend.

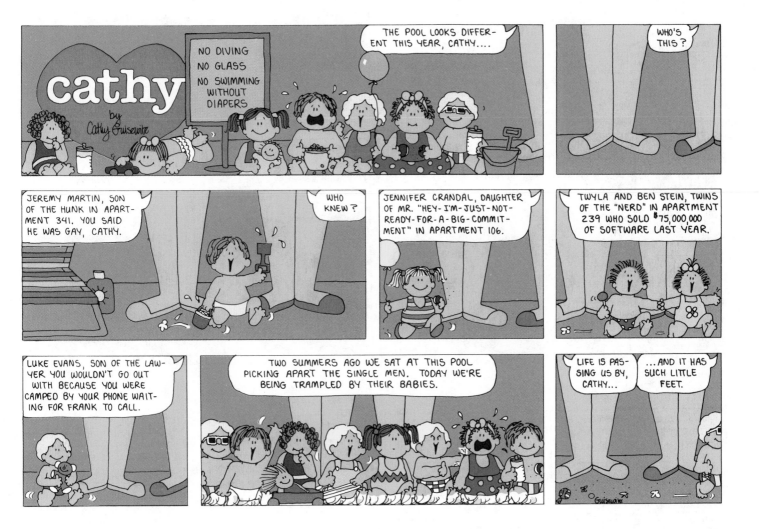

Like so many of life's great events, the Return to Motherhood Trend was timed to exactly coincide with the moment that many of us had not only pledged to put off motherhood for at least another ten years, but had actively made the sort of commitment to our careers that only left about five seconds a week for a social life. Since the inside of an office was all a lot of us were seeing at that point, it's where we dealt with it—and a thousand conflicting feelings about it—first.

Since Andrea spent the previous several years militantly campaigning for Cathy's complete independence from ANYTHING HAVING TO DO WITH MEN, it seemed appropriate to have Andrea be the first in line to the altar.

She planned her wedding like a marketing strategy, and ultimately met and married a man she met on an interactive computer modem program.

Andrea approached pregnancy with the passion, research, and tenacity typical of a generation of overachievers.

It was 1986. Women had been in the work force long enough to know how to rise above the pack with power performance and killer management skills . . . there was a movie star in the White House . . . a "Baby on Board" sticker on every BMW . . . a Sharper Image catalog in every mailbox . . . a free-range chicken with organically grown herbs in every stainless steel, charged-to-a-charge-card-on-a-cordless-phone, pot.

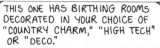

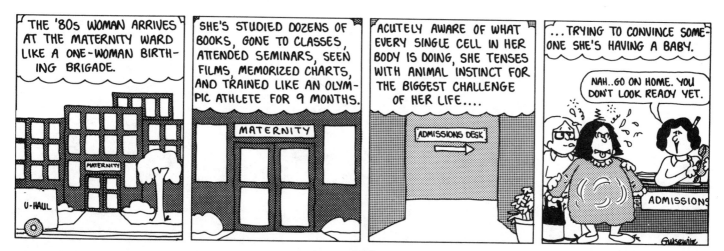

The only thing Andrea hadn't prepared for was the fact there was no maternity leave offered at the company where she worked.

In the past decade, we had quickly moved from the concept of women "choosing" to work to the concept of women having to work just to make ends meet. The "typical American family" of one breadwinner, one homemaker and two children was a luxury almost no one could afford anymore. Ironically, at a time when there were supposedly more options for all women, most women found themselves having to make excruciating choices or—like Andrea—having the choices made for them.

264

Between Andrea's history of being vocal on women's issues and her own experience of having been fired for taking a maternity leave, I felt it was only natural for her to actively campaign for Dukakis, the candidate who supported the same national day-care and parental leave legislation she did, in the 1988 election.

Since none of the many strips I'd done in the past two years on the same subjects had gotten even one negative response, I was a little surprised at the fury that resulted from nine election-related strips. Cathy was dropped for a time from some papers and moved to the editorial page in others. Many papers kept the strip in the comic section but ran stories about the controversy, and published some of the thousands of letters sent by readers who were either thrilled or horrified that Cathy, which was "supposed to just be about women's stuff" had been used to voice a political opinion about women's stuff.

While Andrea dealt with the realities of motherhood, Cathy grappled with it in her own way. Lots of questioning . . .

Occasional loans . . .

And, finally, a bold and brave commitment . . .

I wasn't ready for Cathy to have a baby yet, but was anxious for her to get to experience at least a taste of motherhood. Her maniac puppy, Electra, has given her that. Fueled by a "biologically-ready Grandma" (Cathy's mother will knit booties for anything with feet), Cathy's "mothering" experience has paralleled Andrea's in more ways than I expected.

On the next several pages is a look back at some of the best and worst moments of their first years with their little ones.

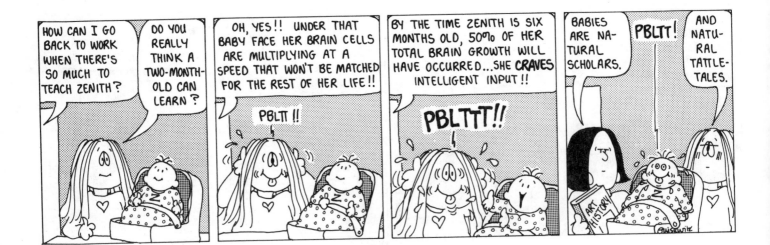

# Epilogue

## 1976

## 1977

## 1978

## 1979

*1984*

*1985*

*1986*

*1987*

_1988_

_1989_

_1990_

_1991_